A Paines Plough
Belgrade Theatre, La
Royal & Derngate, Nort

MY MOTHER'S FUNERAL: THE SHOW

by Kelly Jones

My Mother's Funeral: The Show
by Kelly Jones

Cast

DARREN	Samuel Armfield
MUM	Debra Baker
ABIGAIL	Nicole Sawyerr

Creative Team

Director	Charlotte Bennett
Set and Costume Designer	Rhys Jarman
Lighting Designer	Joshua Gadsby
Sound Designer	Asaf Zohar
Movement Director	Rachael Nanyonjo
Dramaturg	Lauren Mooney
RTYDS Intensive Residency Director (supported by the RTYDS Annie Castledine Award)	Phillippe Cato
Casting Director	Nadine Rennie CDG
Production Manager	Harry Armytage for The Production Office
Company Stage Manager	Roni Neale

A Paines Plough, Mercury Theatre, Belgrade Theatre, Landmark Theatres, and Royal & Derngate, Northampton co-production.

With thanks to Anne and James McMeehan Roberts for their support of the production of *My Mother's Funeral: The Show*.

The commissioning of *My Mother's Funeral: The Show* was enabled by a grant from the New Play Commission Scheme, a project set up by the Writers' Guild of Great Britain, UK Theatre and the Independent Theatre Council, and funded by Arts Council England, the Theatre Development Trust and donations from actors, directors, playwrights and producers, and supported by the Mercury Theatre Colchester.

My Mother's Funeral: The Show was developed with the support of the National Theatre's Generate programme.

KELLY JONES (Writer)
Kelly Jones is a gay working-class playwright and neo-burlesque performer from Dagenham. She is the winner of the BBC Wales Drama Award 2014, alumni of the Emerging Playwrights' Group at the Bush Theatre, BBC Drama Room 20/21, Mercury Theatre's East England Voices and Orange Tree Theatre Writers Collective. Recent credits include: *Ghost Stories by Candlelight* (HighTide/Shakespeare's Globe); *When You See Me* (Scottee & Friends); *Room to Escape* (NTW/BBC Arts); *Comma* (Sherman Theatre); *Garden Paradiso* (Mercury Theatre); *Snout* (Òran Mór); *Blud* (The Otheroom). *My Mother's Funeral: The Show* is a recipient of the Writers' Guild New Play Commission.

CHARLOTTE BENNETT (Director)
Charlotte Bennett (she/her) joined Paines Plough as Joint Artistic Director alongside Katie Posner in August 2019. For Paines Plough Charlotte has directed *Reasons You Should(n't) Love Me* by Amy Trigg (winner of the Women's Prize for Playwriting) which premiered at Kiln Theatre in May 2021 before embarking upon a UK tour of seventeen venues and returning to the Kiln in 2022, and *Run Sister Run* by Chloë Moss (Sheffield Theatres/ Soho Theatre). Previously she was Associate Director at Soho Theatre where she led the new writing department, developing artists and commissions and programming. For Soho Theatre, she directed *Whitewash* by Gabriel Bisset-Smith, *Happy Hour* by Jack Rooke, curated a six-month off-site arts festival in Waltham Forest and led playwriting competition the Verity Bargate Award. Prior to this she was Artistic Director of Forward Theatre Project, an artists' collective she founded. For Forward Theatre Project she made and directed new plays which toured nationally inspired by working in partnership with different communities around the UK and at venues including the National Theatre, York Theatre Royal, Northern Stage, Derby Theatre, Live Theatre and The Lowry. As a freelance director she has worked extensively for Open Clasp Theatre Company creating new plays inspired by women in the North-East and she held the role of Producer for theatre company RashDash for 4 years where she toured experimental new theatre around the UK.

RHYS JARMAN (Set and Costume Designer)
Rhys Jarman was one of the winners of the 2007 Linbury Biennial Prize. In 2017, he won the One Drama Award from the Shanghai Modern Drama Valley for his designs for *The Dreamer* with Gecko and Shanghai Dramatic Arts Centre. In 2019, his designs for Gecko's *The Wedding* was exhibited at the V&A as part of Staging Spaces exhibition. Recent designs include: *Strategic Love Play* (Paines Plough); *I, Daniel Blake* (UK tour); *Kin* (Gecko/ National Theatre); *Police Cops: The Musical* (New Diorama); *The Secretaries* (Young Vic); *A View from the Bridge* (York Theatre Royal); *Henry V*, *The Tempest*, *The Borrowers* (Grosvenor Park Open Air Theatre); *Future Bodies* (HOME); *Nassim* (Bush Theatre). Work for Gecko includes: *A Little Space* (Mind the Gap/Gecko); *The Wedding*, *The Dreamer* (co-production with Shanghai Dramatic Arts Centre); *Time Of Your Life* (co-production with the BBC); *Institute*, *Missing*.

JOSHUA GADSBY (Lighting Designer)
Joshua Gadsby is a lighting designer and creative collaborator working across theatre, dance and live art. He regularly co-designs set, costume, and lighting with designer Naomi Kuyck-Cohen. Recent lighting designs include: *Twine* (The Yard); *Dugsi Dayz* (Royal Court); *Liberation Squares* (Nottingham

Playhouse/UK tour); *Kiss Marry Kill* (Dante or Die, UK tour); *Dreaming and Drowning* (Bush Theatre); *New Beginning* (Queen's Theatre Hornchurch); *Mom, How Did You Meet the Beatles?* (CFT); *Who Killed My Father* (Tron/UK tour); *The Beauty Queen of Leenane* (Theatre by the Lake); *Alice in Wonderland* (Mercury Theatre, Colchester).

ASAF ZOHAR (Sound Designer)
Asaf Zohar is a composer and sound designer for theatre, film and television. He trained at the Royal College of Music. Theatre includes: *Ballet Shoes* (National Theatre); *Macbeth* (site-specific: London/Liverpool/Edinburgh, Washington); *God of Carnage* (Lyric Hammersmith); *Some Demon, Here, The Silence and the Noise* (Papatango); *Sessions, Whitewash* (Soho Theatre); *Peter Pan Reimagined* (Birmingham Rep); *The Shape of Things, Disruption* (Park Theatre); *Dennis of Penge* (Guildhall/Ovalhouse/Albany Deptford); *Sorry, You're Not A Winner* (Bristol Old Vic/Theatre Royal Plymouth); *Nanny* (Bristol Old Vic); *Captain Amazing, The Bleeding Tree, The Bit-Players, Romeo and Juliet* (Southwark Playhouse); *Waiting for Anya* (Barn Theatre); *Bright Half Life* (King's Head); *Wild Country* (Camden People's Theatre); *The Goose Who Flew* (Half Moon Theatre); *The Shadowpunk Revolutions* (Edinburgh Fringe). Television includes: *Reggie Yates: Extreme Russia*; *Reggie Yates: Race Riots USA*; *Reggie Yates: Extreme UK*; *Reggie Yates: Extreme South Africa* and *Dispatches: Taliban Child Fighters*, in addition to in-house work for Virgin Media and various media companies. His film work has been shown at Cannes, BAFTA, Edinburgh and Encounters festivals.

RACHAEL NANYONJO (Movement Director)
Rachael Nanyonjo is an Offie-nominated choreographer, movement director and director working across theatre, film and TV. Theatre includes: *Boys from the Blackstuff* (Liverpool Royal Court/National Theatre/Garrick Theatre); *Moby Dick* (UK tour); *Misty* (West End/The Shed, New York); *Dumbledore is so Gay* (Southwark Playhouse); *Uncle Vanya* (Theater Dortmund); *The P Word* (Bush Theatre); *The Tempest* (Shakespeare's Globe); *Purple Snow Flakes and Titty Wanks* (Royal Court); *Bernstein's Mass* (Royal Festival Hall, Southbank Centre); *Shebeen* (Nottingham Playhouse/Stratford East); *Trouble in Mind* (National Theatre). Television includes: *Love at First Sight* (Netflix); *The Following Events are Based on a Pack of Lies* (BBC/Sister productions).

LAUREN MOONEY (Dramaturg)
Lauren Mooney is a writer, producer and dramaturg. Since 2015 she has co-run award-winning Kandinsky Theatre Company, where her credits include acclaimed productions at New Diorama Theatre, the Royal Exchange Theatre, Manchester and the Schauspielhaus in Vienna, as well as extensive UK touring and international transfers, including to the Schaubühne, Berlin. Beyond Kandinsky, she works in dramaturgy, script editing and writer development across theatre and audio, including for Clean Break (where she co-edited their monologue collection *Rebel Voices*), LAMDA, Big Finish and Wales Millennium Centre. She is a graduate of the Royal Court Playwriting course.

PHILLIPPE CATO (RTYDS Intensive Residency Director, supported by the RTYDS Annie Castledine Award)
Phillippe Cato (he/him) is a freelance director, dramaturg, and singer-songwriter. As director: *Finding Olokun* (Stanley Arts) As assistant director: *The Big Life* (Stratford East). As dramaturg: *Always Maybe the Last Time* R&D (Royal Court); *The Merry Wives of Windsor* R&D (Shakespeare's

Globe); *Hot in Here* (UK tour/Gate Theatre); *The Importance of Being Earnest* (ETT/Leeds Playhouse/Rose Theatre Kingston/UK tour); *Bogeyman* (Edinburgh Festival Fringe); *Avalanche* R&D (Bloom Theatre). In January 2023, Phillippe co-founded Telluric., with producer Wayne Glover-Stuart, a company with the mission to tell representative LGBTQIA+ stories and narratives from global perspectives via theatre productions. @phillippecato

NADINE RENNIE CDG (Casting Director)
Paines Plough work includes: *Orphans* by Dennis Kelly, *Run Sister Run* by Chloë Moss. Nadine has over twenty years' experience as a casting director for theatre. She was in-house Casting Director at Soho Theatre for fifteen years; working on new plays by writers including Dennis Kelly, Bryony Lavery, Arinzé Kene, Roy Williams, Philip Ridley, Laura Wade, Hassan Abdulrazzak, Steve Thompson and Oladipo Agboluaje. Since going freelance in January 2019 Nadine has worked for theatres and companies across London and the UK, including Gate Theatre, Royal Court, Arcola Theatre, Orange Tree Theatre, Leeds Playhouse, Sheffield Crucible, Pilot Theatre, Fuel Theatre, National Theatre of Wales, Northern Stage, King's Head, Finborough, Wales Millennium Centre, Kiln Theatre, Park Theatre, Theatre503, HOME Manchester, Pleasance Theatre London, Almeida, Lyric Hammersmith, Hampstead and Minack Theatres. She also has a long-running relationship with Synergy Theatre Project as their Casting Director/Consultant. TV includes: BAFTA-winning *Dixi* (BBC), casting the first three series. Nadine is a member of the Casting Directors Guild and currently sits on the Committee.

HARRY ARMYTAGE for The Production Office (Production Manager)
Harry Armytage studied at LIPA, graduating in 2014. After graduating, he worked in a variety of roles across the theatre, opera and events sectors, working in areas such a scenic construction, operations management, and lighting (technical and lighting design roles). Since then, he has held full-time production management roles within producing houses such as the Watermill Theatre, Garsington Opera, and most recently as Technical & Production Manager of the Barn Theatre, Cirencester. He has looked after UK national tours, and transfers into London from regional producing houses. He is now working in a project management role for The Production Office, on a wide range of projects.

RONI NEALE (Company Stage Manager)
Roni Neale is a stage manager and theatremaker from Dorset, working nationally. They live with their partner and two cats, Aria and Hector. Theatre includes: *Hungry* (Soho Theatre/Edinburgh Fringe Festival); *English* (RSC/Kiln Theatre); *Cowbois* (RSC/Royal Court); *Manic Street Creature*, *Indecent Proposal*, *Brother*, *Public Domain*, *The Fabulist Fox Sister*, *DNA* (Southwark Playhouse); *Housemates Festival* (Brixton House); *Charlie and the Chocolate Factory*, *Hedwig & the Angry Inch* (Leeds Playhouse); *Dear Elizabeth*, *Shubbak Festival* (Gate); *Ride*, *Foxfinder*, *Pressure* (West End); *Billionaire Boy* (UK tour); *Horrible Christmas* (Alexandra Palace); *Dealing With Clair* (Orange Tree).

SAMUEL ARMFIELD
Samuel Armfield graduated from the Guildhall School of Music and Drama. Theatre includes: *An Enemy of the People* (West End); *Sing Yer Heart Out for the Lads* (Chichester Festival Theatre). Television includes: *Big Boys* S2 (Channel 4); *FBI: International* (CBS).

DEBRA BAKER
Theatre includes: *Frankie and Johnny in the Clair de Lune* (The Bridge Theatre, Brussels); *This Might Not Be It* (Bush Theatre); *Glacier* (Old Fire Station, Oxford); *Orlando* (West End); *SAD* (Omnibus Theatre, Clapham); *The Witchfinder's Sister* (Queen's Theatre, Hornchurch); *Big Guns* (Yard Theatre); *Home Theatre* (Theatre Royal Stratford East); *Radiant Vermin* (Soho Theatre/New York). Television includes: *Supacell* (Netflix); *Dr Who* (BBC/Disney); *It's A Sin, Home* (Channel 4); *King Gary, Holby City, Call the Midwife, Doctors, Close to the Enemy* (BBC1); *Coronation Street* (ITV1); *Sliced* (UKTV); *The Five* (Sky1), *Phoneshop* (Ch4). Film includes: *Re-Awakening, Body of Water, London Road, Lie Low, 90 Minutes, Night Bus*. Radio includes: *The Shell Seekers, Dr Faustus, Home Front, Charles Paris, Jane Eyre, The Forsyte Saga, The Periodic Table, Inspector Chen, To Hull & Back* (BBC Radio 4).

NICOLE SAWYERR
Nicole Sawyerr is an actor and director from north-west London. She trained at ArtsEd. Theatre includes: *Wuthering Heights* (China Plate/Royal & Derngate); *Don Quixote* (Perth Theatre); *Road* (Northern Stage); *Much Ado About Nothing* (RSC); *Beneath the City* (Birmingham Rep); *Hansel & Gretel: Fairytale Detectives* (Theatr Clwyd); *The Croydon Avengers* (Ovalhouse/ Maya Productions); *The Fairy Tale Revolution, The Words Are Coming Now, Boom, Do You Pray* (Theatre503); *Where De Mangoes Grow* (The Pleasance, London); *Aladdin* (Perth Theatre); *Miss-Able* (Arcola Theatre); *Beam Me Upperthorpe* (Migration Matters Festival/Paperfinch Theatre); *After Orlando* (Finborough Theatre); *Those Who Trespass, The Path* (HighTide Theatre Festival). Film, television and voiceover includes: *EastEnders* (BBC); *The Bin Bag Girls* (Short Film); *Athena* (Netflix). Directing credits include: *Do We Have To Go Home?* (Omnibus Theatre/ Unshaded), *The Importance of Being Earnest* (dir. Scott LeCrass, Play in the Park Productions).

 **Paines Plough**

Hello! We're Paines Plough. We're a theatre company that specialises in new writing, led by Joint Artistic Directors Charlotte Bennett and Katie Posner. As a touring company dedicated to new writing, we discover, develop and empower writers and share their explosive new stories with audiences all over the UK and beyond.

Founded in 1974, we have worked with over 500 playwrights including Sarah Kane, Dennis Kelly, Miriam Battye, James Graham, Nathan Bryon, Kae Tempest, Vinay Patel, Mike Bartlett, Chloë Moss, Zia Ahmed and Anna Jordan.

'An essential part of the UK's new writing ecology… its nationwide place in that has only grown in recent years.'

Lyn Gardner, *Stage Door*

Our plays are nationally discovered and locally heard. We tour our shows to over 30,000 people annually, including in Roundabout – a state-of-the-art, in-the-round pop-up theatre – which tours around the country with us and takes residency at Summerhall in Edinburgh during the Fringe Festival in August.

Alongside producer Ellie Keel, we co-founded the Women's Prize for Playwriting in 2019 to redress the imbalance of stories being told on our national stages, and have co-produced two of the winners so far: *Reasons You Should(n't) Love Me* by Amy Trigg and *You Bury Me* by Ahlam.

In 2023, we launched Tour the Writer, a nationwide writer development programme to provide opportunities to writers and budding writers around the country.

'The lifeblood of the UK's theatre ecosystem.'

Guardian

Paines Plough

Joint Artistic Directors & CEOs	Charlotte Bennett & Katie Posner
Executive Director	Jodie Gilliam
Producer	Ellie Fitz-Gerald
Marketing and Audience Development Manager	Manwah Siu
Assistant Producer	Mrinmoyee Roy
Administrator	Hannah Churchill
Press Representative	Bread and Butter PR

Board of Directors
Ankur Bahl, Corey Campbell, Lauren Dark, Asma Hussain, Helen Perryer, Farha Quadri, Carolyn Saunders, Kully Thiarai (Chair).

Paines Plough Limited is a company limited by guarantee and a registered charity.

Registered Company no: 1165130
Registered Charity no: 267523

Paines Plough Offices, Stockroom, 38 Mayton Street, London, N7 6QR

office@painesplough.com
www.painesplough.com

Follow @PainesPlough on Twitter
Follow @painesplough on Instagram
Like Paines Plough at facebook.com/PainesPloughHQ
Donate to Paines Plough at justgiving.com/PainesPlough

MERCURY

Mercury Theatre is the artistic powerhouse in the East – a vital, vibrant, welcoming centre of culture for the people of Colchester, Essex and beyond. The award-winning theatre presented in our auditorium and in our studio transforms and enriches the lives of our community. Through our Mercury Productions and Mercury Originals we produce world-class theatre, reinventing familiar stories and conjuring up bold, new ones. Our talent development programme seeks out fresh voices and stories that encourage people to see through the eyes of others. The Mercury's participation programmes connect communities and celebrate creative potential by providing people with everyday opportunities to be artistic and innovative.

A producing and receiving house with 530 seats in the theatre and a capacity of 96 in the studio, the newly (2021) refurbished Mercury is accessible throughout and boasts a thriving café-bar, dance studio, rehearsal space, participation space and impressive backstage workshop.

Following the major renovation in 2021, Mercury was awarded a BREEAM Very Good certificate, placing it in the top 25% of public buildings in the UK for environmental standards. In 2021 the Mercury was profiled by Theatre Trust as a model of good practice in the UK.

The Mercury was established in 1937, is registered Charity Number 232387 and receives regular investment from:

Premier Partners

mercurytheatre.co.uk
@MercuryTheatre
#MercuryForAll

Executive Director	Steve Mannix
Deputy Executive Director	Deborah Sawyerr
Senior Producer	Dilek Latif
Producer	Jenny Moore
Literary Associate	Kenny Emson

My Mother's Funeral: The Show continues a series of published plays by writers who are alumni of our Mercury Playwrights scheme, whose work has gone on to be produced in our studio as Mercury Originals.

Other Mercury Originals available in print include:
Sirens by Kenny Emson
Evelyn by Tom Ratcliffe
Kabul Goes Pop by Waleed Akhtar
Bindweed by Martha Loader

THE BELGRADE THEATRE COVENTRY

As the largest theatre in Coventry and a leading regional producing theatre, the Belgrade has a broad, varied programme.

Popular musicals and entertainment sit happily alongside progressive, critically acclaimed new drama. Our two spaces, B1 and B2, stage exciting productions and events for families, couples, individuals, first timers and confirmed theatregoers.

As a publicly subsidised independent charitable trust, we also support health and education and build skills and talent in the region. Everything we do is with, by and for our local communities.

Some of our productions are fresh takes on well-loved stories. Others explore new ground – and have never been told before. To them all, we bring warmth, openness and collaboration, creating new community connections and encouraging different perspectives. By sharing the city's diverse stories, the Belgrade brings people in Coventry together. We call this co-creation.

Led by CEO Laura Elliot and Creative Director Corey Campbell, the Belgrade is realising its ambitious plans to build on the Theatre's rich history of inclusion. Born out of the post-Second World War spirit of peace and reconciliation, and named with gratitude for the Serbian capital's gift of timber to build a new theatre, the Belgrade has offered a warm welcome to visitors since 1958.

Whether you're visiting the Belgrade for a show, a business event, or simply for tea, cake and a chat with friends, this unique sense of welcome is still unmissable.

Executive and Senior Management Team

CEO	Laura Elliot
Interim CEO (Maternity cover)	Neil Murray
Creative Director	Corey Campbell
Director of Finance	Neil Harris
Director of Production & Operations	Adrian Sweeney
Head of Communications	Ray Clenshaw
Director of Producing and Co-Creation	Adel Al-Salloum

www.belgrade.co.uk

LANDMARK THEATRES

Landmark Theatres, born from Selladoor Venues is a portfolio of regional venues in North Devon and Peterborough receiving a wide variety of arts and cultural opportunities for local communities including major touring productions, high profile live music acts, big-name stand-up comedy, dance, superb theatre and new writing. We also produce high quality Theatre, Drama and Family productions including our annual family Pantomime in Peterborough.

We pride ourselves on an in-depth understanding of the locations in which we operate. Working in areas of lower cultural engagement across the UK. We are respecting and responsive to local priorities, deliver innovation and work in partnership to empowering our communities. We deliver a breadth of creative activities and ways in which our communities can engage whether that be as an audience member, participant, decision maker or through developing talent.

info@landmarktheatres.co.uk
01271 316523
www.landmarktheatres.co.uk

Chief Executive Jo Gordon
Artistic Director Jesse Jones

Royal & Derngate, Northampton is the main venue for arts and entertainment in Northamptonshire and one of the major regional producing theatres in the country, with its acclaimed Made in Northampton work touring nationally and internationally.

The theatre was nominated for Theatre of the Year in The Stage Awards 2022. Eight of its productions transferred to London and the West End in 2019, with *The Worst Witch* winning the 2020 Olivier Award for Best Family Show and *Our Lady of Kibeho* being nominated for the 2020 Olivier Award for Outstanding Achievement in an Affiliate Theatre. The adapted screenplay from Royal & Derngate's original play commission of *The Pope* was nominated for Best Adapted Screenplay at the Academy Awards as Netflix's *The Two Popes*.

Looking ahead, the theatre is excited to be presenting a new stage adaptation of *The Jolly Christmas Postman*, as well partnering with Paines Plough on *My Mother's Funeral: The Show* and with the Rose Theatre in Kingston for a new stage adaptation of Kazuo Ishiguro's *Never Let Me Go*.

Other recent Made in Northampton productions have included Ralph Fiennes in the world premiere stage adaptation of T.S. Eliot's *Four Quartets* which transferred to the West End and was made into a film, a new version of Joe Penhall's *Blue/Orange*, touring co-productions of *Animal Farm* and *Othello* with the National Youth Theatre, a brand new musical *Gin Craze!* by April de Angelis and Lucy Rivers, the world premiere stage adaptation of *Mog The Forgetful Cat*, the national and international tour of Agatha Christie's *And Then There Were None* and most recently Spymonkey's *The Frogs* and Simple8's *Moby Dick*.

The venue also presents a diverse range of visiting productions on both the Derngate and Royal stages, featuring musicals, dance, comedy and music, and its two-screen cinema presents the best in world, independent, British and mainstream film.

Royal & Derngate's nationally recognised Creative Engagement programme works with schools, families and communities in Northamptonshire and beyond, and its Generate artistic development programme regularly supports hundreds of regional artists each year.

Box Office 01604 624811
www.royalandderngate.co.uk

Facebook: /royalandderngate
X: @royalderngate
Instagram: @royalderngate

MY MOTHER'S FUNERAL: THE SHOW

Kelly Jones

Acknowledgements

With huge thanks to: Charlotte Bennett for directing the play so beautifully. Thank you for your belief, openness, and for allowing me to tell the story I want to tell. Dramaturg Lauren Mooney for helping me tame this beast. Everyone at Paines Plough. Evie King and Ruth Arnold for your generosity. My incredible agent Maeve Bolger. Everyone who has supported the idea from the beginning – Dilek Latif, Ryan McBryde, the Mercury Theatre Colchester. The New Play Commissions Scheme. Deirdre O'Halloran and the Bush. National Theatre Studio Generate. All actors and creatives who have read and informed the play at various stages – Grace Duggan, Joanna Bacon, Doreene Blackstock, Lilly Driscoll, Shane Zaza, Thomas Coombes, Fanta Barrie, Rebekah Murrell, Ashna Rabheru, Jake Davies, Kenny Emson and Ella Hickson. Special thanks to the cast of this production: Sam Armfield, Debra Baker and Nicole Sawyerr, who have brought so much joy, humour and talent to the rehearsal room; and have brought the play to life with such beauty and truth, I am in awe. My friends and family. My mum, for making me strong. My dad, for always making me laugh. My writing ride-or-dies the Defectors (RA, AG, IL, TW). All the partners making this happen – Mercury Theatre, Belgrade Theatre Coventry, Landmark Theatres, Royal & Derngate, Northampton; and finally: Nick Hern Books for publishing this edition.

K.J.

*To Lucy and Zeta,
without whom none of this would be possible.
Love you x*

Characters

ABIGAIL WALLER, *twenties*
MUM, *fifties*
GRAVEDIGGER ONE
GRAVEDIGGER TWO
DIRECTOR
FUNERAL DIRECTOR
DARREN WALLER, *thirties*
BANK
DIFFERENT BANK
CREDIT CARD
LOANS
ACE
MATE
DATE
CASH FOR STUFF
MORTICIAN
ACTOR
SET DESIGNER
TECHIE
COUNCIL

The actor playing Abigail should always play Abigail. All other characters are doubled as below:

DARREN/DIRECTOR/GRAVEDIGGER/DIFFERENT BANK/ LOANS/MATE/CASH FOR STUFF

MUM/ACTOR/GRAVEDIGGER/FUNERAL DIRECTOR/ MORTICIAN/BANK/CREDIT CARD/LOANS/ACE/DATE/ SET DESIGNER

All three actors should be active and onstage all the time; even if they are not scripted in a scene, they should be preparing for their next one in full view.

Note on Text

A forward slash (/) indicates overlapping dialogue.

An ellipses (…) means an unfinished thought or space, not as defined as a pause.

A dash (–) indicates an interruption.

Words in [brackets] should not be spoken.

Punctuation is used to dictate rhythm and pace.

A line that ends without punctuation indicates incompleteness. In lines with a full stop (.) it should be played.

Note on Play

A basic funeral in 2024 costs over £4000.

Funeral costs have risen 126% in the last twenty years.

7% of all funerals conducted are by local councils.

www.sunlife.co.uk/funeral-costs

This text went to press before the end of rehearsals and so may differ slightly from the play as performed.

GRAVEDIGGERS ONE *and* TWO *are digging a hole in the ground. Mud piling high, portable radio blaring; they keep digging.*

GRAVEDIGGER ONE. It's all relative mate

GRAVEDIGGER TWO. Is it?

GRAVEDIGGER ONE. Course. Some places have bombs for breakfast.

GRAVEDIGGER TWO. I know...

GRAVEDIGGER ONE. Kids get snatched, cancer, the economy's fucked, there's people living in doorways

GRAVEDIGGER TWO. ...all of that, still.

GRAVEDIGGER ONE. Pays the bills

GRAVEDIGGER TWO. That's debatable

GRAVEDIGGER ONE. I don't mind it

GRAVEDIGGER TWO. Hand on heart?

GRAVEDIGGER ONE. I would if I had one mate.

GRAVEDIGGER TWO. I'm not like that

GRAVEDIGGER ONE. Give it a few months.

GRAVEDIGGER TWO. I couldn't drink my tea this morning

GRAVEDIGGER ONE. I don't drink tea, on burial days

GRAVEDIGGER TWO. The milk was off. Except it weren't, but somehow my brain had me convinced. Then 'off milk' became 'off people', now I'm not sure I'll ever drink tea again

GRAVEDIGGER ONE. First-time nerves that's all

GRAVEDIGGER TWO. Do you ever think about who they are?

GRAVEDIGGER ONE. I don't take it seriously mate

GRAVEDIGGER TWO. It is serious though.

GRAVEDIGGER ONE. Not for us

GRAVEDIGGER TWO. What if it was someone you knew?

GRAVEDIGGER ONE. Who?

GRAVEDIGGER TWO. A neighbour or…?

GRAVEDIGGER ONE. I'd know

GRAVEDIGGER TWO. How would ya?

GRAVEDIGGER ONE. Nothing gets past me

GRAVEDIGGER TWO. Yet here you are.

GRAVEDIGGER ONE. And here you are, three foot deep

GRAVEDIGGER TWO. I couldn't afford a funeral.

GRAVEDIGGER ONE. Failing to prepare is preparing to fail, my ol' man used to say.

GRAVEDIGGER TWO. Don't you think it's sad though?

GRAVEDIGGER ONE. Cancer's sad. Fucking West Ham losing, that's sad.

GRAVEDIGGER TWO. Four today, five tomorrow

GRAVEDIGGER ONE. Could be anyone in there though. Murderer, nonce, Tory

GRAVEDIGGER TWO. In Dagenham?

GRAVEDIGGER ONE. Be surprised mate

GRAVEDIGGER TWO. No way.

GRAVEDIGGER ONE. We get all sorts

GRAVEDIGGER TWO. Probably some old dear, died alone, no savings, no generous relatives.

GRAVEDIGGER ONE. We all end up the same.

GRAVEDIGGER TWO. They did a documentary when Jimmy Savile died

GRAVEDIGGER ONE. One big ready meal, mate.

GRAVEDIGGER TWO. And a drama with Steve Coogan. I won't get Steve Coogan.

GRAVEDIGGER ONE. Wouldn't want him.

GRAVEDIGGER TWO. Wouldn't know. All I'm sayin' is…

GRAVEDIGGER ONE. It's a box mate

GRAVEDIGGER TWO. It ain't though, is it?

GRAVEDIGGER ONE. Parcel for the earth. Deliveroo for the worms. Mrs Worm bulk-ordering her Mills and Boons. Fucking *Fifty Shades*.

GRAVEDIGGER TWO. Woteva mate.

GRAVEDIGGER ONE. Muddy cow. Ha.

…

GRAVEDIGGER TWO. Should we say something?

GRAVEDIGGER ONE. Ain't allowed.

GRAVEDIGGER TWO. Wouldn't know.

GRAVEDIGGER ONE. He wouldn't hear us anyway.

GRAVEDIGGER TWO. Suppose not.

GRAVEDIGGER ONE. Come on. Let's go get you a cuppa.

GRAVEDIGGER TWO. I am gaspin'

GRAVEDIGGER ONE. Same mate. Same.

House lights flicker. They exit.

MUM (*fifties*) *enters. She waits, and waits, and…*

Beat.

ABIGAIL WALLER (*twenties*) *stands looking around the space.* DIRECTOR *approaches.*

DIRECTOR. Abigail Waller, there she is.

ABIGAIL. Thanks for seeing me.

DIRECTOR. Drink? We've got a lovely elderflower pressé

ABIGAIL. Water's fine, ta. Especially at such short notice

DIRECTOR. I always make time for my favourite writers…

ABIGAIL. I do appreciate it

DIRECTOR. …when they show up unannounced

ABIGAIL. I have been emailing, but no one replied

DIRECTOR. If anything we should be appreciating you

ABIGAIL. Not that you have to

DIRECTOR. For your time, your brilliant ideas

ABIGAIL. I'm no Shakespeare

DIRECTOR. Without artists like you, Abigail

Beat.

ABIGAIL. Artists like me

DIRECTOR. Storytellers with interesting things to say about worlds we wouldn't get to know about otherwise.

ABIGAIL. That's what I thought

DIRECTOR. I was only telling someone yesterday what you told me about the trauma of having never lived somewhere with stairs before

ABIGAIL. I don't think I said that

DIRECTOR. Word for word

ABIGAIL. Cos, I do have stairs and a lift. They're not mine but I don't lie awake at night longing for my own. Of all the things wrong, I'm not like, why don't we all have our own set, ya know.

DIRECTOR. Tell me why you're here, Abs

Beat.

ABIGAIL. Right. Well.

DIRECTOR. I'll tell you why. Your beautiful play. *Astro-mite*.

ABIGAIL. I know it should have been on your desk sooner

DIRECTOR. Every play on my desk should have been there sooner

ABIGAIL. There is no excuse for handing in late

DIRECTOR. Every writer hands in late

ABIGAIL. I don't

DIRECTOR. You did

ABIGAIL. I am grateful

DIRECTOR. You've said

ABIGAIL. Being commissioned by you was one of the best days of my life, cos I have loved this theatre ever since I came here with my mum and saw it snow onstage.

DIRECTOR. I've told you before, paper from the rafters Abs.

ABIGAIL. Even so, I have dreamt of creating that level of magic onstage, on that stage ever since

DIRECTOR. Do you know why we commissioned you?

ABIGAIL. You liked my idea

DIRECTOR. A good idea isn't what makes someone commissionable

ABIGAIL. It's not?

DIRECTOR. Tell me about your debut, *Rage, Dagenham Beat.*

ABIGAIL. It wasn't my best

DIRECTOR. No, but it was real, raw, urgent, brave

ABIGAIL. I shouted at the audience for over an hour

DIRECTOR. It made me uncomfortable as a white middle-class cis-het able-bodied man

ABIGAIL. Can't go anywhere these days

DIRECTOR. So, when you pitched *Astro-mite*, I was excited, hungry for the same level of angst. Of course I was nervous. Does a play about gay termites in a Space Dagenham, scream 'our audiences'?

ABIGAIL. It's not really about gay termites though

DIRECTOR. Probably not, but I wasn't about to pass on the most exciting voice I'd heard in years. What is the point of holding the purse strings if I can't pay writers to write?

ABIGAIL. Again, so grateful.

DIRECTOR. You may have seen we're making some changes here, Abs. Exciting changes. Asking ourselves what will allow us to keep supporting artists like you.

ABIGAIL. Cool.

DIRECTOR. It's simple, all I wanted when I was a young artist was clarity

ABIGAIL. Clarity, really?

DIRECTOR. I was going to wait to do this but seeing as you're here. We have decided, we will not be moving forward with your play *Astro-mite*.

Beat.

ABIGAIL. Sorry, what?

DIRECTOR. Sorry, Abs

ABIGAIL. You said it was beautiful.

DIRECTOR. We love the bug stuff.

ABIGAIL. The bugs are only a metaphor

DIRECTOR. It's *Bug's Life* meets Kafka meets *Star Trek*

ABIGAIL. Not what I was going for.

DIRECTOR. We love it Abs, but it's not right for us, now

ABIGAIL. I don't mind waiting

DIRECTOR. Or any time soon.

ABIGAIL. I don't understand

DIRECTOR. We have a duty here Abs, to bring in audiences or we don't exist. Whilst your play is good, it is as I feared, not what our audiences want, any more.

ABIGAIL. Stuff like this sells out here all the time

DIRECTOR. When it's existing IP, Abs

ABIGAIL. You said I could write what I want

DIRECTOR. I said through your unique lens

ABIGAIL. This is through my lens

DIRECTOR. It's set in space, no one in space is on benefits

ABIGAIL. It's fiction.

DIRECTOR. Fiction doesn't sell any more. Our audiences want real stories, told by real people, a chance to see into a world unlike their own, in every way, to both challenge what they believe about people like you and confirm it. They want you, your story, not bugs in space, understand?

ABIGAIL. I am not that sort of writer.

DIRECTOR. You were in your debut

ABIGAIL. I was going through a break-up

DIRECTOR. All I'm sayin' is, there is no shame in writing what you know, especially when what you know gets bums on seats.

Beat.

It's out of my hands

ABIGAIL. Ain't this your theatre?

DIRECTOR. It belongs to the artists really.

ABIGAIL. Sorry, I will still get my fee, won't I, if you don't want the play? The contract says unless you want to put it on, I won't get paid the full fee.

DIRECTOR. Sorry, Abs. I've got to go. Lovely to see you. Send us some new ideas, when you've got them. Try setting the next one a little closer to home. Maybe make us feel bad. Audiences love that.

Beat.

DIRECTOR *exits.*

FUNERAL DIRECTOR *enters and passes* ABIGAIL *a brochure.*

FUNERAL DIRECTOR. This is our 2024 brochure, with all our packages. Costs on the left are standard. Costs on the right are your extras: fancier coffins, caskets, urns.

ABIGAIL. Is it meant to sound like I'm a booking a holiday?

FUNERAL DIRECTOR. If it's not listed let us know and we can try and get it in for you

ABIGAIL. Where will I find brass handles?

FUNERAL DIRECTOR. They're an extra. If you are shopping around and you do find a cheaper package elsewhere, we will price-match, not on the oak, or we won't make any money. Did you and the deceased get a chance to discuss what she wanted?

ABIGAIL. Mum wanted to be buried.

FUNERAL DIRECTOR. Lovely. Is there a family plot?

ABIGAIL. I don't think so.

FUNERAL DIRECTOR. We can arrange that, it will cost extra, not the arranging, the plot

ABIGAIL. How much?

FUNERAL DIRECTOR. Providing a local cemetery has space two thousand five hundred.

ABIGAIL. Okay.

FUNERAL DIRECTOR. Have you had a chance to register the death?

ABIGAIL. Does that make it cheaper?

FUNERAL DIRECTOR. Sadly, no. It is a legal requirement, you will be fined if you don't. Once you've registered and claimed the body you are legally responsible for the cost of the admin, disposal and service. Any questions?

ABIGAIL. Do you have another brochure?

FUNERAL DIRECTOR. Are you looking for something specific?

ABIGAIL. More in budget

FUNERAL DIRECTOR. What's your budget?

ABIGAIL. I don't have one.

FUNERAL DIRECTOR. Top-end burial you're looking ten thousand plus

ABIGAIL. What about the lower end?

Beat.

FUNERAL DIRECTOR. I see, for people on the lower end I recommend this

ABIGAIL. Is there any movement on that price, or?

FUNERAL DIRECTOR. We don't do discounts, I'm afraid. It does cover all your fees, embalming, viewing the body.

ABIGAIL. I could see her…?

FUNERAL DIRECTOR. If you want to. We find it brings people a lot of closure. We need twenty-five-per-cent deposit to book, balance the day before. We take cash, credit card…

ABIGAIL. Can you hold it till the end of the week? I'm waiting to be paid

FUNERAL DIRECTOR. Unfortunately not. We do offer a payment-plan option.

ABIGAIL. Okay. I'll do that.

FUNERAL DIRECTOR. All our payment plans are subject to a full credit check

ABIGAIL. I see. Are there any payment options that don't involve checks or money upfront?

FUNERAL DIRECTOR. Sadly no. Some people ask family to contribute…

Beat.

DARREN (*thirties*) *enters.*

DARREN. I don't want any part of it, Pebbles

ABIGAIL. She's our mum, Dal

DARREN. She ain't been mine for years

ABIGAIL. You're the one who chose to move out

DARREN. I mean it, none of it.

ABIGAIL. We've got to book a funeral, Dal

DARREN. Do you know how expensive funerals are Pebbles?

ABIGAIL. I do now.

ABIGAIL. Four grand. We need two grand each

DARREN. Two grand! I ain't even got two quid

ABIGAIL. We'll have to think of something

DARREN. Can't you ask your rich artist mates?

ABIGAIL. I don't hang out with the rich ones

DARREN. You need to start

ABIGAIL. Will you ask Dad?

DARREN. I ain't had money from him in years

ABIGAIL. You can tell him what it's for

DARREN. He already knows, Pebbles. Sorry.

Beat.

ABIGAIL. We must know someone.

DARREN. Ain't no 'we'.

ABIGAIL. You ain't getting out of it, Dal

DARREN. It's been years since I seen her

ABIGAIL. Whose fault is that?

DARREN. She knew where I was.

ABIGAIL. What about me? Why didn't you come find me when you heard?

DARREN. You know how it is

ABIGAIL. I thought I did.

Beat.

DARREN. I felt weird.

ABIGAIL. Weird ain't the normal response when your mum dies.

DARREN. Well, I did. Right or wrong. When I heard, I felt weird, indifferent

ABIGAIL. Fucking hell, Dal.

DARREN. See. I'm best out of it

ABIGAIL. You ain't leaving it to me.

DARREN. Why you so bothered?

ABIGAIL. I can't claim her until I can afford her

DARREN. You can't afford her

ABIGAIL. When I claim her, I am responsible for her

DARREN. Leave her in the morgue

ABIGAIL. I am not abandoning Mum in that place, Darren.

DARREN. Don't sound like you got much choice.

ABIGAIL. Ask Dad.

DARREN. He ain't got it Pebbles.

ABIGAIL. Woteva he can spare

DARREN. I dunno wot you're not getting.

ABIGAIL. You ain't asked him

DARREN. He ain't got nothing. Trust.

ABIGAIL. What about a loan?

DARREN. Are you stupid?

ABIGAIL. Provident, in his name. I'd pay him back.

DARREN. Do it in your own name.

ABIGAIL. I've tried, they won't.

DARREN. Shouldn't have let her fuck your credit, should ya?

ABIGAIL. Darren. Please.

Beat.

DARREN. Ain't she got life insurance?

ABIGAIL. No.

DARREN. Savings?

ABIGAIL. Do you?

DARREN. What about her benefits?

ABIGAIL. They've stopped them already

DARREN. What about yours?

ABIGAIL. I don't get them cos I'm self-employed

DARREN. They can help though; council can bury her.

ABIGAIL. In a shared grave in the poor bit of the cemetery, lovely

DARREN. It's free

ABIGAIL. I'm not putting my mother in a grave with strangers.

DARREN. There's no shame in it

ABIGAIL. Do you know they call it a 'pauper's burial'?

DARREN. Snobs do. So, unless you're a snob

ABIGAIL. I don't trust Barking Council to fix a leaky tap, let alone bury Mum.

DARREN. You sound just like her.

ABIGAIL. Good.

DARREN. I'm fine with the council doing it

ABIGAIL. It's not what she wanted

DARREN. My bad, pass me her giro and I'll book the horses.

ABIGAIL. She didn't want horses cos they shit everywhere

DARREN. How you gonna find four grand?

ABIGAIL. I'll find it.

Beat.

DARREN. Look, do yourself a favour, ring the council, tell them you can't afford it. Then go get what you want out that flat before they lock it up; and move on.

ABIGAIL. I don't care about the flat, Darren.

DARREN. I've got to go; pick Maisie up from her mum's. Leave me out of it, yeah?

He walks away

ABIGAIL. Dal, don't you wanna know how I felt when I found out?

DARREN. Save it Pebbles. Might be worth something.

DARREN *exits.*

ABIGAIL *makes a series of phone calls.*

BANK. Hello, the bank.

ABIGAIL. I want to apply for a loan

Beat.

DIFFERENT BANK. Hello, a different bank.

ABIGAIL. I want to apply for a loan

DIFFERENT BANK. Do you have a guarantor?

Beat.

CREDIT CARD. Credit-card company

ABIGAIL. I would like to increase my credit-card limit

CREDIT CARD. Occupation?

ABIGAIL. Freelance theatremaker

The line goes dead.

Hello?

Beat.

LOANS. Loans4u.

ABIGAIL. I want to apply for a loan

Beat.

LOANS. Loans, Loans, Loans

ABIGAIL. I want to apply for a –

Beat.

ACE. Arts Council England

ABIGAIL. How long does it take for a project grant to come through?

Beat.

MATE. Mate!

ABIGAIL. Mate.

I will pay you back

MATE. I haven't got it, sorry

Beat.

ABIGAIL. Fraud. Totally wiped my savings. If you could sub me…?

DATE. Sorry, who is this?

ABIGAIL. Abigail Waller, we met on Hinge

Beat.

CASH FOR STUFF. Cash for Stuff

ABIGAIL. I need to sell my laptop

CASH FOR STUFF. I can give you one-fifty cash or two hundred store credit

ABIGAIL. It's worth way more

CASH FOR STUFF. I'll also throw in a free pen

ABIGAIL. I don't want a free pen. I want a coffin for my mum

CASH FOR STUFF. Please hold

ABIGAIL. Don't put me on hold, please don't put me...

DARREN *enters and intercuts* MORTICIAN.

A voicemail.

DARREN. Do you know how expensive funerals are Pebbles?
You can't afford her.

Phone the council

How are you going to find four grand?

Save it Pebbles, it might be worth something...

MORTICIAN. Hello Ms Waller, King's Hospital Mortuary. Sorry to bother you at this difficult time. / I can see we have Linda with us. I'm checking in to see how arrangements are progressing. / We do still need you to formally 'claim the body', sooner the better, we are limited on space. / If Linda isn't claimed and we don't hear from you within twenty-one days, we will have to refer her to the state. / If you could give me a call back to discuss, it'd be greatly appreciated. Again, sorry for your loss.

DIRECTOR *appears.*

DIRECTOR. Abigail Waller, twice in one week

ABIGAIL. Thanks for making time, again

DIRECTOR. Drink?

ABIGAIL. I'm not stopping, ta. I wonder if I can run an idea past you.

DIRECTOR. Work it into a page, a few scenes and we'll set something up

ABIGAIL. It's sort of a now idea.

DIRECTOR. I'm a bit pushed Abs

ABIGAIL. I understand, but I think it's exactly what you're looking for. What I've been looking for. Through my lens. Gritty, real, urgent, benefits, misery, trauma, class, pain story.

DIRECTOR. I'm listening.

Beat.

ABIGAIL. So, the main character has recently lost her mum

DIRECTOR. We've already done a dead mum play this year, Abs.

ABIGAIL. Not like this. See this character / thought…

DIRECTOR. What's her name?

ABIGAIL. I dunno yet.

DIRECTOR. Maybe come back when you're more prepared, Abs

ABIGAIL. Stacey.

DIRECTOR. Tell me about Stacey

ABIGAIL. Stacey thought we all ended up the same when we die. Cremation or burial.

DIRECTOR. When my dog died, we got him made into a tree

ABIGAIL. Exactly. Cremation, burial, tree, that's what we all assume

DIRECTOR. My aunt was made into a paperweight

ABIGAIL. Stacey doesn't have money to turn her mum into paperweight. Sadly. In Stacey's story there's no will, no estate, no inheritance, no money for even the most basic funeral.

DIRECTOR. Why can't she get a loan?

ABIGAIL. Her credit's shit from when she used to knock Britannia and Capital One. There is some help from the government, but it only covers a tenth of the cost; and it's not likely she'll get it until after the funeral.

DIRECTOR. Right. Why do you think an audience will care?

ABIGAIL. Cos she's lost her mum

DIRECTOR. That's not enough to sell seats, Abs. You know that. Tell me, why our audience will care?

Beat.

ABIGAIL. Stacey has been on benefits her whole life. As a child she was taken to sign on with her mum. At school she was made to stand in a different queue for her lunch, she was the only child in her class who didn't have a Furby, branded trainers, her own set of stairs. Her home is owned by the council, her food, her clothes, now, if she can't find the money, her mum will be too.

Beat.

DIRECTOR. Oh, that's good. I like it. It feels complex. The lengths we all go for dignity. Very social media age. Wow.

ABIGAIL. I would like to start Monday

DIRECTOR. Why so soon?

ABIGAIL. Before someone else gets there.

Beat.

DIRECTOR. Monday.

ABIGAIL. Do I need to invoice again, for my fee, or…?

DIRECTOR. Oh, were you thinking you'd be paid?

ABIGAIL. I was hoping so.

DIRECTOR. I was thinking this would come under your original commission for *Astro-mite.*

ABIGAIL. So, I still only get paid if you decide to put it on.

DIRECTOR. It's pretty standard.

ABIGAIL. When will you know if you want to put it on?

DIRECTOR. Why the rush?

ABIGAIL. It's such a now idea.

DIRECTOR. Get me pages and I'll see.

DIRECTOR *exits.*

ABIGAIL *steps up to the mic. She goes to speak but can't. She walks away. She tries again, still doesn't speak. She omits a noise into the mic. She walks away. She tries again.*

ABIGAIL. Hello… would the owner of the blue Ford Escort…

She starts again.

Alright. I'm Abigail. Playing Stacey, Stace, in the play, the performance…?

She starts again.

Hello. I'm Stacey. Alright. I'm Stace. I'm fuckin' twenty-four, from fuckin' Dagenham and I'm working class. Although you probably already knew that from my swearing and the tiny weights inside my face. This is a 'something' about me and…

She starts again.

This is a 'thing' about Mum, my mum, my beautiful mum, recently she… she… she… I'm an imposter, I'm an imposter, I'm an imposter, I'm an imposter, I'm an imposter.

She takes a break. MUM *appears, a memory.*

MUM. Say 'Christmas Theatre trip 2016', Abigail

ABIGAIL. Mum. People are looking.

MUM. Good. (*Beat.*) Aww it does suit you, being in here.

ABIGAIL. You always say everything suits me

MUM. Didn't when you showed me those silver trousers last week

Beat.

I can see it, you, up there, your plays, like this

ABIGAIL. I don't have 'plays'

MUM. What was those pages you showed me the other night?

ABIGAIL. I was only messing about

MUM. Don't give the characters names if you're only messing about

ABIGAIL. Anyone can come up with a name. Not like this. This is proper

MUM. Who said you ain't proper?

ABIGAIL. I couldn't do this, I ain't got nothing to say, like, my life ain't that interesting

MUM. It is to me.

ABIGAIL. You have to say that.

MUM. Oh. You could do about that time we went Canvey and you fell in sea.

ABIGAIL. I don't think that's the sort of thing they'd be after, Mum

MUM. It's a great story

ABIGAIL. No it's not.

MUM. Don't see enough dramas set in Canvey

ABIGAIL. Why don't you write one?

MUM. I'll leave it to the professionals, Abigail

ABIGAIL. I'm not good enough to be a professional.

MUM. Good enough to me.

Have some self-belief. You're talented.

...

I'll let you borrow my Debbie Harry story if you like

ABIGAIL. That weren't Debbie Harry

MUM. There, were ya?

ABIGAIL. Why would Debbie Harry be in a pub in Dagenham?

MUM. Shh. It's starting.

ABIGAIL *steps back up to the mic, she starts again.*

I wake up, in a dark chasm

A deep fissure in the earth's surface

A chasm, a gorge, a gully, a gap, a hole

I'm accompanied by a thesaurus

I awaken.

Rousing and rising, inciting, eyes fighting the glue holding them still in my head.

Someone is pushing me

Forcing me.

Shepherding me towards the sole exit from this fleshy pink palace that I have called home for nine months.

I am being born yet to who, to whom? Yet to *whom* I don't know. I don't get to choose. Neither does she.

I've heard the outside. Smelt it. Tasted it.

Tasted what she tastes.

Charlie Red and cigarettes; Friday chippy-tea

I am not wot she will be expecting. For I am the sort that travels through the cracks, a societal tick, cards stacked.

Beat.

Her pushing increases. I try to resist, stop and list all the ways she could possibly receive me, but it's too late. I'm out and...

I see her. My mum. My beautiful mum. Nine days ago she died. Welcome to *My Mother's Funeral: The Show*. Lights.

DARREN *enters*.

DARREN. Spoke to the council then?

ABIGAIL. Nah. I'm paying.

DARREN. Blimey. You win the lottery?

ABIGAIL. I got it coming, from work.

DARREN. Four grand from the chippy. I'm in the wrong job.

ABIGAIL. My proper job. I'm writing a play.

DARREN. The one about the gay bugs in space?

ABIGAIL. Different one.

DARREN. I like that one – (*Quotes.*) Take me to your gay bar

ABIGAIL. They don't say that

DARREN. Should. What's this one about then?

ABIGAIL. Stuff.

DARREN. Wow and that's worth four grand?

ABIGAIL. Yeah, it is.

DARREN. Tell me.

ABIGAIL. Don't act bothered

DARREN. Who came to your reading when she couldn't?

ABIGAIL. She was working.

DARREN. Even if she weren't. Go on.

ABIGAIL. It's about a young woman whose mum's died.

Beat.

DARREN. Bit close to home, ain't it?

ABIGAIL. Called writing wot you know.

DARREN. There's writing wot you know and there's writing wot you found out the other day

ABIGAIL. It'll be good for me. Cathartic.

DARREN. Will it?

ABIGAIL. Don't worry, you're off the hook.

Beat.

DARREN. Sounds depressing, who'd wanna watch that.

ABIGAIL. People round here do go the theatre, Darren

DARREN. The only time I know anyone from round here to go in there is to have a shit, Abigail

ABIGAIL. I go in there and I'm from round here

DARREN. You're different

ABIGAIL. What's that supposed to mean?

DARREN. You're from round here, I know that cos I'm your brother.

ABIGAIL. And it's true.

DARREN. You don't act like you are though. The way you talk, dress

ABIGAIL. The way I dress?

DARREN. Artsy.

Beat.

Why don't you do about Canvey when you fell in the sea or when you won the talent contest in Yarmouth.

ABIGAIL. This is how all the proper writers do it, Dal

DARREN. You seemed proper at your reading

ABIGAIL. Fiction doesn't sell any more.

DARREN. Then how come George Lucas is so rich?

ABIGAIL. Not as rich as a Kardashian.

Beat.

DARREN. Are they making you, cos it's true? If you need me to have words, you know I don't need an excuse to deck a posh cunt

ABIGAIL. They don't know it's true.

DARREN. They don't know your mum's just died?

ABIGAIL. It's none of their business

DARREN. What you gonna do when they start criticising it?

ABIGAIL. Who said they're gonna?

DARREN. Giving you notes, changing things

ABIGAIL. I know what I'm doing, Dal

DARREN. You better. I don't want it getting left to me. Cos if this goes tits-up, I ain't sorting it, Pebbles. Trust, I'll leave her there

ABIGAIL. I have sorted it.

DARREN. How is this sorting it?

ABIGAIL. I'm writing about Mum.

Beat.

DARREN. Don't put me in it

ABIGAIL. How much is it worth?

DARREN. I mean it, Pebbles.

Beat.

ABIGAIL. Now it's sorted, we should think about clearing the flat.

DARREN. There you go with that 'we' again

ABIGAIL. You're the only one I know with a van, Dal.

DARREN. No.

ABIGAIL. I'll give you petrol and I'll get us some chips

DARREN. Chips?! Even if they were platinum, Pebbles

ABIGAIL. I dunno how long I got before the council lock it up.

DARREN. I ain't doing it.

ABIGAIL. Don't you wanna see if there's anything you want?

DARREN. Ain't nothing for me in there, Pebbles.

Beat.

ABIGAIL. There is for me. It'll only take a few hours

…

Forget it. I've done everything else on my own. Don't see why I should expect anything from my brother.

She goes to leave

DARREN. Fine, I can spare a few hours, to run things down the tip and carry boxes, if it'll help, but know I ain't doing it for her.

ABIGAIL *goes back to writing, she steps up to the mic.*

ABIGAIL. My mum. Canning Town born and bred, she left when the council kicked out all their tenants and sold their flats to their mates. As a result, Mum both raged at the system and was shit scared of it. She was rehomed in a high-rise in Dagenham. That high-rise is where she met the sperm that made me, where I grew up and she became my soul mate.

I know everyone says their mum is the greatest but mine… If she was a song, she'd be 'Bohemian Rhapsody', if she was weather, she'd be a rainbow, if she was clothes, she'd be a chunky-knit jumper. When my goldfish died, she organised a wake. When I told her I was gay, she told me, no man was good enough for me anyway and bought me a Sarah McLachlan CD. She loved me and the feeling was mutual.

Ten days ago she…

DIRECTOR *interrupts.*

DIRECTOR. It's a little frothy, for my taste, Abs

ABIGAIL. Is that bad?

DIRECTOR. It's not what we're trying to make.

Beat.

ABIGAIL. I'm open to suggestions.

DIRECTOR. A play like this shouldn't be frothy, it should be fire.

ABIGAIL. I can do fire.

DIRECTOR. It should feel like her words hurt her, hurt us whilst making us feel completely safe that it'll never be us. Understand?

ABIGAIL. Not really.

DIRECTOR. It needs to be gritty, Abs

ABIGAIL. Right, gritty, I can do gritty

DIRECTOR. Her mum has just died

ABIGAIL. I know.

DIRECTOR. I don't think you do

ABIGAIL. I promise I do.

DIRECTOR. I know it can be hard writing things you haven't experienced; but a show like this needs to be specific, or it won't work.

ABIGAIL. I was only exploring ideas

DIRECTOR. I have a suggestion. Give me Mum.

ABIGAIL. What'd you mean?

DIRECTOR. Give me Mum and Stacey together

ABIGAIL. I thought we were doing the solo thing.

DIRECTOR. Try not to think about the show

ABIGAIL. Isn't that not wot I'm meant to be doing?

DIRECTOR. Free yourself up, spend today thinking about your own mum, really tune in to the reality of Stacey's situation.

What you'd do? How you'd feel? Put them on the page
together, see what happens. Tomorrow, we'll workshop some
material, go from there. Sound good?

ABIGAIL. Great. Thanks. I wondered, if you had any more
thoughts, on whether you want it yet, or is it too early to tell?

DIRECTOR. I probably need to see more than ten pages, Abs

ABIGAIL. How many more?

DIRECTOR. Look, why don't you try this, and we'll chat

He exits, a voicemail.

MORTICIAN. Hello, Ms Waller, this is King's Hospital
Mortuary. We understand this is a difficult time, but if you
could give us a call about Linda, we'd greatly appreciate it.

ABIGAIL *is on the mic.*

ABIGAIL. Historically when mums [die], things happen.
Arrangements. I know, cos this is what happened when my
nan went. She had a burial, big floral letters spelling 'Gran',
'Mum', 'West Ham'. Loads of guests. People spilling out of
the church. You could wade in the tears. It was paid for by an
old boyfriend who still held a torch. Lucky Gran. Historically
when people go, this is what happens, family, friends, an old
flame. Eleven days ago, my mum… and, well, things never
happen like they're meant to for me and my mum.

MUM *enters singing 'Happy Birthday'.*

MUM. Open ya presents

ABIGAIL. You didn't have to.

MUM. I wanted to.

ABIGAIL. OMG, did you go to H&M?

MUM. Barking Market

ABIGAIL. Thanks Mum. I love it

MUM. I love you, babe

ABIGAIL. Love you too, Mum.

Beat.

MUM. Go on then, put it on.

MUM *steps up to the mic.*

X Factor Champion 2014 is…

ABIGAIL. Mum

MUM. Crowd goes wild, confetti, the works. Well, go on.

ABIGAIL. I'd like to thank Simon, Louis, Cheryl, Tulisa. My mum, who is sat front and centre. She will always be front and centre to me, no matter what.

She sings. Something cringe.

MUM. I want you to sing at my funeral, babe

ABIGAIL. Why'd you have to ruin it?

MUM. Don't tell me you ain't thought about it?

ABIGAIL. It's morbid.

MUM. I have. I want people crying, not a few single tears, proper crying. The sort where they have to choose between crying and breathing cos it ain't possible to do both at the same time. I want everyone in black, none of this bright-colour nonsense, it ain't Gay Pride. I want a sea of flowers, so many cards it empties Clintons.

ABIGAIL. Who said you're having flowers?

MUM. I better, or I'll haunt you. I will haunt you.

ABIGAIL. I'm scared

MUM. I don't want horses cos they shit everywhere. I wouldn't mind doves or a few bleached pigeons but don't go to any trouble.

ABIGAIL. I am not bleaching a pigeon for you

MUM. And I wanna be buried cos cremations ain't arf boring. I like the fuss of a burial, it's a bit more involved, immersive, as you theatre lot call it.

ABIGAIL. That's not what that means

Beat.

MUM. Now, the coffin, I ain't fussy about linings

ABIGAIL. Good, cos all my money's gone on flowers and cards

MUM. But I would prefer oak, with brass handles. Nanny wanted brass, but they were out of stock. She'd hate if I had brass, but least it'd give us something to fight about when I get up there. Or down, depending

ABIGAIL. Stop.

MUM. And make sure whatever you dress me in is ironed, it is a funeral for goodness' sake, I don't want people thinking, lovely service but her blouse weren't arf creased.

ABIGAIL. No one will see it anyway.

MUM. I will. Don't you dare send me off with a creased blouse, I mean it

ABIGAIL. Alright.

MUM. You'll have to do a speech, your brother won't, then I doubt he'll be there. Make sure you keep it short, none of those funny words you like to use. It makes people switch off babe

ABIGAIL. I wouldn't wanna bore anyone at your imaginary funeral

MUM. Only imaginary now

ABIGAIL. I don't like it

MUM. We have to have these chats, darling.

ABIGAIL. What if I go before you?

MUM. Bloody better not. You are clumsy. Oh don't, my head's thinking of all sorts

ABIGAIL. See.

MUM. Sorry, I'll stop. Quickly. I do want my final words to be something brilliant. Like ''Asta la vista' or 'Gillian'… Gillian?

ABIGAIL. Gillian.

MUM. Or 'Gillian, Gillian, Gillian, don't forget the pie in the oven!'

ACTOR *steps out of the role of Mum.*

ACTOR. Sorry Abigail, who's Gillian?

ABIGAIL....

DIRECTOR. Gillian is Stacey's nickname.

ABIGAIL. Sorry. No. There is no Gillian.

Beat.

'Gillian don't forget the pie' is Mum's idea of famous last words.

ACTOR. So, I, Angela, know I'm dying

ABIGAIL. No more than we all do

DIRECTOR. Remind us how she died, Abs?

ABIGAIL. In hospital

Beat.

It was her heart.

ACTOR. And am I aware of my heart condition in the scene.

ABIGAIL. No.

She's just being morbid, you know, the way parents are when they reach late fifties

I can change it, if it's not clear...

DIRECTOR. No, it's powerful stuff, Abs

ACTOR. Such an incredible scene.

ABIGAIL. Yeh?

DIRECTOR. This is what I've been waiting for.

ABIGAIL. Well, I tried what you said, think about the show, don't think about the show

ACTOR. It's so desperate and bleak.

ABIGAIL. Is it?

DIRECTOR. Especially that moment when Stacey asks Angela to stop, and she goes on to deliver those famous last words

ACTOR. Asking Gillian to take the pie out the oven and not Stacey is brutal. I could cry.

DIRECTOR. It's really gritty, Abs

ABIGAIL. Gritty?

ACTOR. Urgent.

DIRECTOR. Brave.

ABIGAIL. Funny?

Beat.

ACTOR. I didn't get funny

DIRECTOR. We're watching Stacey get abused by a shopping list we know she can't afford. Who would laugh at that?

ABIGAIL. I thought the pigeon line was quite funny

ACTOR. I found the pigeon heartbreaking.

DIRECTOR. The imagery alone.

ACTOR. The fact that later in the play we might see Stacey actually attempt to bleach a pigeon in order to give me doves at my funeral, is devastating

ABIGAIL. I don't think Mum is being serious

ACTOR (*as* MUM). I'm being deadly serious, Stacey

DIRECTOR. How else is she going to supply doves?

ABIGAIL. She doesn't know, yet

DIRECTOR. There is no other choice. We know we're going to have to watch her go through with it, then she'll try to release it at the funeral, only to find out it's dead too. It's genius.

ACTOR. I've got goosebumps

ABIGAIL. I think the line's enough, without seeing it

DIRECTOR. I disagree. Tell me something truer to the working-class experience, than watching a woman bleach a pigeon in order to provide doves at a funeral she can't afford

ABIGAIL. You've got me there.

DIRECTOR. Imagine the audience, collectively willing it to happen then when it does, feeling both elated and guilty for bringing it into existence. It's exactly the sort of story our audiences want, the sort of story you said you wanted to write, isn't it?

ABIGAIL. Yes. (*Beat.*) I been thinking the pigeon should probably be a childhood friend

DIRECTOR. Very *Sophie's Choice.*

ABIGAIL. Exactly. Will she choose the pigeon or her mum…?

ACTOR. Can we talk about Mum?

Beat.

ABIGAIL. What do you want to know?

DIRECTOR. Is she inspired by your own mum, Abs?

ABIGAIL. You did ask me to think about my own

DIRECTOR. She feels very authentic. Even as a middle-class man, I know this woman

ABIGAIL. I wanted her to feel like she could be all of our mums, regardless of class

DIRECTOR. She's that mum we see in Asda

ACTOR. In her dressing gown

DIRECTOR. Screeching at her children by the vodka

ABIGAIL. I can't tell if you're joking.

Beat.

ACTOR. She's obviously very manipulative

ABIGAIL. How?

ACTOR. I want a sea of flowers, so many cards it empties Clintons. I want you *so* upset you have to choose between crying and breathing

ABIGAIL. Who doesn't want that at their funeral?

ACTOR. I haven't once acknowledged how expensive emptying Clintons might be. How exhausting it'll be for her to cry that hard

ABIGAIL. Stacey loves Mum

DIRECTOR. Love won't pay for a sea of flowers, Abs

ABIGAIL. I know.

Beat.

ACTOR. Can I check, I haven't left any money, at all?

ABIGAIL. There isn't any money

DIRECTOR. There must be some money, though.

ABIGAIL. She gets her benefits

DIRECTOR. Why can't Stacey use that?

ABIGAIL. It's ninety quid a week and they've stopped them already.

ACTOR. And there's no will or savings or funeral plan?

ABIGAIL. There isn't any money.

Beat.

ACTOR. So, I am really setting you up to fail in this moment, aren't I?

DIRECTOR. God that's good

ACTOR. Demanding when I have no intention of providing

ABIGAIL. Where does it say that?

DIRECTOR. Well, she doesn't say she wants a pauper's burial.

ABIGAIL. Cos, she doesn't.

DIRECTOR. Beggars and choosers

ABIGAIL. Who said anything about beggars?

ACTOR. Surely if I loved Stacey, I wouldn't want her to get into debt

ABIGAIL. She does love Stacey

ACTOR. Asking for doves, doesn't feel like love

DIRECTOR. Yes, if she loved Stacey, she'd tell her to phone the council, surely?

ACTOR. I am so selfish.

ABIGAIL. Sorry. I'm still not understanding how she is selfish. For me, in this moment Angela is being generous. She is telling Stacey what she wants; and doing it using their love language, which is to play. She really loves Stacey and Stacey loves her. They are just an ordinary mother and daughter, that's what makes it so sad, I think.

ACTOR. You haven't written me like that

Beat.

DIRECTOR. That also doesn't sound very dramatic.

ACTOR. I say, I want you to have to choose between crying and breathing

ABIGAIL. That's her humour, if you'd met my mum

ACTOR. I see. Is that what it is?

DIRECTOR. Are you worried about her seeing this, Abs?

ABIGAIL. She won't see this.

DIRECTOR. Cos we can make her different enough that she won't know it's her, if that'd make you more comfortable

ABIGAIL. It's not her

ACTOR. You said she was your inspiration.

ABIGAIL. Not like this.

DIRECTOR. Okay. Why don't we break there?

ACTOR *exits.*

ABIGAIL. I thought you wanted me to write truthfully. Through my lens.

DIRECTOR. This is your lens.

ABIGAIL. It feels like someone else's, fiction

DIRECTOR. Nothing wrong with fiction

ABIGAIL. You told me fiction doesn't sell any more

DIRECTOR. Depends on the fiction

ABIGAIL. You told me to write what I know; this sort of parent isn't one I know

DIRECTOR. Look, Abs, I understand your nervousness, but everything I am telling you is to make her believable, to our audiences, so you can succeed. This is all excellent stuff. We love Angela's manipulative, selfish nature, as you have written it. I'd encourage you to lean into it, more, if anything. I'd love you to dig into the pain, Abs

ABIGAIL. I'm not sure Stacey has it.

DIRECTOR. Was Stacey with her when she died?

ABIGAIL. No.

DIRECTOR. Quite a big thing to miss. Maybe try and think about that. How did Stacey feel when she found out? When was the last time Stacey spoke to her? Saw her?

ABIGAIL. I'm sure I'll be able to think of something.

DIRECTOR. Good. Bring us some pages tomorrow and we can work through it. And have some self-belief, Abs. You're talented.

ACTOR *steps up to the microphone.*

MORTICIAN. Ms Waller, this is King's Hospital, we still haven't heard from you. If you could give us a call back, as soon as you get this.

ABIGAIL *and* DARREN *put things in boxes.*

DARREN. There's more boxes in the van, different sizes, big, small, medium.

…

I've done us a playlist, I didn't know what you're into any more, so it is mostly rain sounds and a bit of garage; and Maisie made us a packed lunch, it's out of paper but I thought it might be nice to look at when we're finished. She said to say hello.

Beat.

She's with her mum tonight, so, I ain't got to be back. If you fancied, I could see if our Nintendo is still on top of the wardrobe, couple of goes of *Mario Kart* for old times' sake?

…

There's no rush, I told ya council won't come round here this time of night; and I'm alright.

Well, I'm here.

Beat.

I read it's best to go section by section, pack the bits you want first, then anything else you can bin or charity shop. Not that you have to bin anything, although I dunno what you're gonna do with fifty Rod Stewart posters.

…

I'll leave them for you to sort, when you're ready

ABIGAIL. Bin them.

DARREN. Don't you wanna flick through, see if there's any you want? We've got time.

ABIGAIL. I've still got work to do tonight.

DARREN. Surely, they can let you have a night off to clear your mum's flat.

Beat.

I forgot. Sorry. Do you want me to ring and tell them you've got the shits?

ABIGAIL. I'd rather get it done.

Beat.

DARREN. Okay.

...

So, you been alright?

...

Been work today, or?

...

My work let me finish early today, for this

...

They're good like that. If I ever need to pick Maisie up, or... Did I say she said hello?

ABIGAIL. Hello.

DARREN. She'd love to see you soon. We know you're busy.

I could make us some dinner, real food, not paper, if you fancied

I tried to explain to her where I was going today. She wanted to come. We'd never get it finished. I did promise, I'd bring her something back, if that's alright. Something of mine.

ABIGAIL. Take what you want.

DARREN. Like my football trophies or swimming badges.

If Linda kept them. Something I can tell her about, from childhood, something cool. I don't have much of that.

ABIGAIL. I said, take what you want, Dal

Beat.

DARREN. She's becoming a right chatterbox, like you, at that age.

I used to have to bathe my ears in warm water after babysitting you, Pebbles

…

She keeps asking me questions.

About us, and Linda.

Mostly Linda.

How come they never met.

She asked me this morning about her favourite colour.

Couldn't believe I didn't already know.

'I know my mummy's favourite colour.' Leopard-print ain't a colour, Mais

…

I told her I'd ask you.

…

Pebbles.

…

You're the Linda expert

ABIGAIL. Can we knock the 'Linda' chat on the head?

DARREN. I'm only calling her by her name

ABIGAIL. I'd rather not talk about her, tonight.

Beat.

DARREN. Yeah, right.

ABIGAIL. There's a lot to get through and it's slowing us down

DARREN. Something I said?

ABIGAIL. I told you: I've got work to do

DARREN. Can't you do it tomorrow?

ABIGAIL. It doesn't work like that

DARREN. I thought you were self-employed

ABIGAIL. I thought you weren't interested

DARREN. I didn't say that.

ABIGAIL. Okay.

DARREN. Stop being weird.

ABIGAIL. I'm not the one being weird

DARREN. Normally, you don't shut up about her

ABIGAIL. Now I do

Beat.

DARREN. You do remember this is the only night I'm free this week

ABIGAIL. Yep.

DARREN. After tonight, I can't come back here, nor can you

ABIGAIL. Why can't I?

DARREN. It's been over a week; council won't leave it much longer.

…

So, if there's things you wanna say…

ABIGAIL. Things I want to say?

DARREN. With me here.

ABIGAIL. There's nothing I want to say with you here.

DARREN. I don't want you to regret it

ABIGAIL. I'll be fine.

DARREN. Regret can eat you alive, Pebbles

ABIGAIL. Speaking from experience?

Beat.

DARREN. Is it cos of the play?

ABIGAIL. It's not because of the play.

DARREN. Cos, I did warn you.

ABIGAIL. I told you the reason

DARREN. Work is not a reason

ABIGAIL. It is when it's gonna pay for her funeral.

DARREN. Funeral is only one day, Pebbles

ABIGAIL. I don't know why you're acting like you ain't pleased.

Beat.

DARREN. Why would I be pleased?

ABIGAIL. You never want to talk about her.

DARREN. Not in the way you want me to.

ABIGAIL. Not before, not since.

DARREN. Well, let's talk about her, now

ABIGAIL. Convenient, now I've said I don't want to.

DARREN. I'm being serious, Pebbles.

ABIGAIL. I'm gonna go get some boxes.

Beat.

DARREN. Maisie keeps asking me.

ABIGAIL. Make up a favourite colour.

DARREN. It's not only the colour.

ABIGAIL. Tell her Linda's favourite song was 'Maggie May' and she liked Italian food best.

DARREN. Did she?!

ABIGAIL. Are you joking?

DARREN. I'm asking.

ABIGAIL. Darren, I am currently taking her things, our things and putting them in boxes, and you wanna know her favourite colour?

DARREN. I haven't got anyone else to ask.

ABIGAIL. I don't want to hear it.

ACTOR *interrupts.*

ACTOR. How are you getting on with the new pages, Abi?

ABIGAIL. Good.

DARREN. It's so easy for you.

ABIGAIL. Yeah, it's been a real breeze

DARREN. She liked you, for a start

ABIGAIL. Do you think this saucepan is too good for charity?

DARREN. She didn't like me, Pebbles.

ABIGAIL. Do you know anyone who needs a kettle?

DARREN. Pebbles, why didn't Mum like me?

ABIGAIL. She liked you.

DARREN. No, she didn't.

ABIGAIL. Loved both of us.

ACTOR *interrupts.*

ACTOR. Abi, still working on those –

ABIGAIL. Yep.

DARREN. I know love, Pebbles.

ABIGAIL. She would specially go Asda to get you those little pizzas you liked

DARREN. You liked.

ABIGAIL. She went up the school, when you didn't get a part in the school play

DARREN. That was you.

ABIGAIL. She sent you a card when Maisie was born

DARREN. Not to my address she didn't.

ABIGAIL. She has still got your clothes in her wardrobe

If she didn't like you, she wouldn't have kept them. She didn't know you weren't coming back. That ain't my fault and that ain't hers. If anything, you're the one that didn't like her.

DARREN. So, she kept a couple of T-shirts in the back of her wardrobe. Hardly compares to the mountains of 'Abigail' memorabilia. You are everywhere in this flat, I am a speck on a corner of lino in the toilet.

ABIGAIL. What do you expect with the way you treated her?

DARREN. She was my mum.

ABIGAIL. When it suited you.

DARREN. When it suited her.

ABIGAIL. I don't remember that.

DARREN. Then why did she throw me out?

ABIGAIL. She didn't, you left. I remember. You left.

DARREN. No. I didn't.

ACTOR *enters.*

ACTOR. Abi…

ABIGAIL. I'm sending them now.

ACTOR. I wasn't trying to rush you

Beat.

DARREN. Pebbles, do you know how many times I text her? How many times I was this close to knocking on the door?

ABIGAIL. What do you want from me?

DARREN. I want to talk about her

ABIGAIL. I am sick of having to defend her to everyone

DARREN. You don't have to defend her

ABIGAIL. Yes. I do.

DARREN. Can you at least acknowledge that she wasn't the same, for both of us?

ABIGAIL. I…

DARREN. That hurts, Pebbles. I expect it from her but not you. Maybe I should go.

ACTOR *enters.*

ACTOR. Abi, the pages…

ABIGAIL (*to* DARREN). Don't. I want to understand. Tell me how she was, with you.

ACTOR. Love the new sides Abs

ABIGAIL. Thank you.

DARREN. Everything you need to know about who she was for you, is in this flat. In paper clippings, photos, ticket stubs. It's all there. In years to come, when your kids ask you about her, you'll be able to answer without…

ABIGAIL *steps up to the mic.*

ABIGAIL. Everything my little sister needed to know about who Angela was for her, was in that flat. Paper clipping, photos, memories from their days out. She was the centre of her world.

DARREN. Don't you remember her leaving the room every time I entered, asking you to join in, not me.

ABIGAIL. I remember slamming doors

DARREN. Shouting.   ABIGAIL. Shouting

DARREN. I remember her telling you she loved you, a lot

On the mic.

ABIGAIL. I remember Angela telling my sister she loved her a lot. I was jealous, as loudly as she loved her, she hated me ten times louder.

…

She didn't hate you, Darren

Beat.

DARREN. You don't know that. The only person who does, is her and she can't [answer]

ABIGAIL. That's what hurts the most. Angela kept my clothes in her wardrobe, in case I came back. Even from the grave she's fucking with me. Making me question, was it really her? Or was it me?

DARREN. I can't keep ignoring Maisie, Pebbles

ABIGAIL. Then don't.

…

DARREN. What do I tell her?

ABIGAIL. Whatever you want

DARREN. That's the problem. I don't want to, but it's the only way to get her to stop asking

On the mic.

ABIGAIL. I'd love to tell Maisie. Exactly the sort of parent she was, but I don't want her to know that any parent could be like that with their child. I don't want her to wonder whether I'll be like that, one day. Whether all I went through is going to make me like Angela. Twelve days ago, she…

DIRECTOR *interrupts.*

DIRECTOR. It's so sad, Abs.

ACTOR. Heartbreaking

ABIGAIL. Painful?

DIRECTOR. A child, grieving a parent who didn't like them

ABIGAIL. Thank you.

Beat.

ACTOR. I wasn't aware that Stacey was a mother

ABIGAIL. She's not.

DIRECTOR. She talks about a daughter. Maisie?

ACTOR. Bottom of the page

ABIGAIL. That's a mistake

ACTOR. Stacey's gay, isn't she?

DIRECTOR. Yes, did she use a donor or maybe she had a boyfriend once?

ACTOR. Surely, she wouldn't be able to afford IVF?

ABIGAIL. Sorry. There is no Maisie. It's a typo.

DIRECTOR. I like it. Makes the whole play make sense

ACTOR. The need to break the cycle of trauma

ABIGAIL. It's not something I'm interested in

DIRECTOR. That's pain, Abs

ACTOR. I love it.

DIRECTOR. Me too. The fact that Angela couldn't put her own anger aside to meet her only grandchild

ACTOR. I understand now, why I drink.

DIRECTOR. She copes by making art; you cope with Red Stripe

ACTOR. I can play a very convincing drunk

DIRECTOR. Excellent, I'll ask props to send over some bottles

ABIGAIL. Sorry, Angela is not an alcoholic and Stacey is not a mum

Beat.

ACTOR. I thought we decided I was

ABIGAIL. I didn't

DIRECTOR. Given her background

ACTOR. I read alcoholism is more prevalent amongst people on benefits

ABIGAIL. Not everyone on benefits is an alcoholic

DIRECTOR. It's not because she's on benefits

ABIGAIL. So if she was the Fourth Earl of Barking, would you say it?

DIRECTOR. I think the play needs it.

ABIGAIL. You said the play needed pain. I gave you pain

DIRECTOR. Would it help if we changed it from Red Stripe to white wine?

Beat.

ABIGAIL. I don't want to be difficult.

ACTOR. It'd only change a few lines

ABIGAIL. It makes me uncomfortable.

DIRECTOR. Making someone in a story like this an alcoholic is like waiting in a Beckett. The audience will expect it

ABIGAIL. Maybe there's a smaller trope, like, give her a sovereign or…

Beat.

DIRECTOR. I like the drinking

ACTOR. Me too.

ABIGAIL. Look, I love everything else we've come up with so far. Just not this. Maybe she's in recovery, or…

DIRECTOR. That's not as interesting and you know it

ABIGAIL. Surely, we can be cleverer than that

DIRECTOR. It's good drama

ABIGAIL. I'm not interested in outdated tropes. It's not who I am, as an artist

Beat.

DIRECTOR. Do you remember what you said to me, first time we met?

ABIGAIL. Hello?

DIRECTOR. You bowled in and said, I'm Abigail Waller. Council estate

ABIGAIL. So?

DIRECTOR. Why say it?

ABIGAIL. I'm proud of it.

DIRECTOR. You wanted me to pay attention

ABIGAIL. You asked me about myself

DIRECTOR. It's your currency.

ABIGAIL. No.

DIRECTOR. You wanted me to commission you off that alone.

ABIGAIL. I know that doesn't happen for people like me.

DIRECTOR. There you go again. You can't have it both ways.

ABIGAIL. What about the drinking?

DIRECTOR. Remind me how you pitched this idea, again? Benefits, misery, trauma, pain story?

Your job is to make art people want to see. You may not like it but the ones who pay the ticket price will.

Beat.

MORTICIAN. Ms Waller, King's Hospital, Linda can't wait any longer, if you could give us a call…

ABIGAIL *cuts between being on the microphone and being in scenes.*

ABIGAIL. My mum. My beautiful, difficult, my difficult mum

Thirteen days ago, she…

Beat.

DIRECTOR. Let's run it from the top.

ACTOR. Did you want Mum drunk from the very top of the scene?

DIRECTOR. I think so. Try it.

Beat.

ABIGAIL. If she was a song, she'd be… if she was weather, she'd be…

Beat.

MORTICIAN. Ms Waller, this is King's, about Linda, we urgently need to speak to you, if you could give us a call as soon as…

Beat.

ABIGAIL. She didn't like me, and the feeling was, the feeling was…

DIRECTOR. I still need to see more before I decide, Abs

ABIGAIL. How much more?

DIRECTOR. I dunno, twenty pages?

Beat.

ABIGAIL. – feeling was mutual.

Beat.

Historically when people die, things happen.

Arrangements are made. This can only happen if the person left money or had life insurance. Mum couldn't… didn't.

Beat.

DIRECTOR. Can we change it to hamster?

ACTOR. It is the working-class pet

DIRECTOR. Why don't you look at it when you're rewriting the *X Factor* scene?

ABIGAIL. What's wrong with the *X Factor* scene?

Beat.

ACTOR (*drunk*). I want a sea of flowers, so many cards it empties Clintons, Stacey are you listening to me?

ABIGAIL. And I told you I want you sober.

ACTOR. I'll sober up when you promise me, promise me you'll see to me alright?!

Beat.

ABIGAIL. Didn't leave any money, she didn't leave money, but I promised.

Beat.

DARREN. Pebbles, I haven't heard from you. Call me, when you can

Beat.

ABIGAIL. Since then, she has been waiting. Waiting for me, to do something, like I was waiting for her, to do something, to say sorry, I am sorry

Beat.

MORTICIAN. Ms Waller. Your mum has been with us for some time now and we can't leave it much longer, I'm afraid if we don't hear from you by tomorrow, we will refer her to the council

Beat.

ABIGAIL. You said twenty pages.

DIRECTOR. Why don't we talk after the sharing?

ABIGAIL. You didn't say there would be a sharing

DIRECTOR. There is always a sharing

Beat.

ABIGAIL. Since then, waiting, unclaimed. Expecting me to provide, when she didn't. Maisie keeps asking. What's Nanny's favourite colour? When is Nanny's funeral? I can't tell her I don't know the answer to either.

Beat.

SET. What we were thinking, for the design, is your classic council-estate living room. Super glossy. Lots of working-class motifs. Pint glasses, page three cut-outs, ashtrays. Neon coffin. I could get some theatrical dirt samples, to give it that real lived-in feel.

ABIGAIL. Why does it have to be dirty?

SET. Authenticity.

Beat.

DARREN. Pebbles, have I done something? Drop me a text and let me know you're alright, it's Darren

Beat

ABIGAIL. Fourteen days.

Beat.

ACTOR. I've worked since I was sixteen

DIRECTOR. There are jobs, there're always jobs

Beat.

ABIGAIL. Fifteen days.

Beat.

DIRECTOR. They don't help themselves

ACTOR. It's too easy to claim benefits nowadays

Beat.

ABIGAIL. Fifteen days.

Beat.

DIRECTOR. I'm working class, technically

Beat.

ABIGAIL. Fifteen days. Fifteen days. Fifteen days. There are jobs, there are always jobs. If only she'd helped herself.

Beat.

DIRECTOR. Let's look at the pigeon-bleaching scene after lunch

ACTOR. Do you want me stand in for the pigeon?

DIRECTOR. Does that work for you, Abs?

Beat.

ABIGAIL. Sixteen days ago. In death we are the same, that's what they say. The great leveller between the classes.

Beat.

DIRECTOR. Abi was the one who came up with the pigeon

ABIGAIL. Well, I thought what speaks truer to the working-class experience than a woman who is prepared to bleach a pigeon, in order to provide doves at a funeral she can't afford

Beat.

MORTICIAN. Miss Waller. This is a courtesy call to let you know we have now referred Linda to the council…

Beat.

ABIGAIL. Sixteen days.

Beat.

FUNERAL DIRECTOR. I already told you: we need a deposit to book the funeral

ABIGAIL. Can you not make an exception, please?

Beat.

DARREN. Pebbles, why haven't you answered my –

ABIGAIL. Money. Can you –

DARREN. What for?

ABIGAIL. Mum…

DARREN. Don't finish that sentence

ABIGAIL. Please.

DARREN. I've got to go.

ABIGAIL. Darren

DARREN. Leave me alone, Pebbles

Beat.

ABIGAIL. Seventeen days.

Beat.

ACTOR. Love the new stuff with the brother, Abs

Beat.

ABIGAIL. Eighteen days.

Beat.

DIRECTOR. Can we pick up from Stacey and Mum's fight?

Beat.

ABIGAIL. Nineteen.

Beat.

TECHIE. Going dark

ABIGAIL. Sorry, what?

They fiddle with some buttons.

TECHIE. Abi, can you give us your cue line again please?

ABIGAIL. Nineteen days ago, my mum died

TECHIE. And again?

ABIGAIL. Nineteen days ago my mum died

TECHIE. And again

ABIGAIL. Nineteen days ago, my mum died

TECHIE. Last word of the section please

ABIGAIL. Died.

TECHIE. Again

ABIGAIL. Died

TECHIE. One more time

ABIGAIL. Died.

Funeral music begins. ABIGAIL *is given a microphone and begins to sing as a funeral happens around her.*

GHOST MUM *appears. Everything stops.*

MUM. Well, ain't this posh

ABIGAIL. We're not doing that bit yet

MUM. Lights are nice, Abigail.

…

Look at all these people. Do you know they're charging fifteen quid for this?

ABIGAIL. Nothing to do with me.

MUM. Ain't it your show?

ABIGAIL. Not really.

Beat.

Didn't expect to see you here.

MUM. Got bored waiting

ABIGAIL. Don't they have telly in the morgue?

MUM. Signal's surprisingly shit

Beat.

Where you been?

ABIGAIL. Working.

MUM. Telling people how bad I was

ABIGAIL. It's only words.

MUM. In front of people

ABIGAIL. No one we know

MUM. Don't know that

ABIGAIL. No one from round here comes in here

MUM. You're from round here

ABIGAIL. Only time I know anyone from round here to come in, is to have a shit

MUM. Makes it alright, does it?

Beat.

I didn't know I had another granddaughter called Maisie

ABIGAIL. It's fiction

MUM. Is that what these people think?

ABIGAIL. Yes.

MUM. Now I know I didn't raise you stupid

What about Darren, what does he think?

ABIGAIL. Did you want something?

MUM. Thought you'd be pleased to see me

ABIGAIL. I've got writing to do.

MUM. More lying?

ABIGAIL. It's for you.

MUM. How is making out I'm some sort of, for me?

ABIGAIL. Not that part

MUM. Making out you're some sort of…

ABIGAIL. I'm doing it for the money.

MUM. What do we need money for?

ABIGAIL. When have we not needed money?

MUM. Don't make out we were on the streets with our begging bowls.

ABIGAIL. Not far off.

MUM. When?! Our bills always got paid, we always had food, clothes.

ABIGAIL. I remember being at school noticing what everyone else had, except me.

MUM. Unless it was spots, I dunno wot, cos everyone in your class had the same

ABIGAIL. No they didn't.

MUM. Did, all the mums used to go job club together.

ABIGAIL. We were always worrying about money

MUM. You weren't, I made sure of it, Abigail. Don't confuse their version of your life, for your own.

Beat.

ABIGAIL. Well, I'm worrying now

MUM. Why?

ABIGAIL. You didn't leave any

MUM. I left you my Rod Stewart posters, I'm sure they'd be worth a few bob…?

ABIGAIL. Couldn't. I know you couldn't.

MUM. Nah, you'd rather sell me.

ABIGAIL. I don't have a choice.

MUM. There is always a choice.

Beat.

ABIGAIL. You said flowers and brass handles

MUM. I don't want all that.

ABIGAIL. You told me.

MUM. I also said I sang with Debbie Harry down the Roundhouse, babe

ABIGAIL. I promised.

MUM. I didn't ask you to.

ABIGAIL. Did.

MUM. Do you think I would make you promise when I ain't left any money? I wouldn't do that to you or your brother.

…

It's not like I'll even know.

ABIGAIL. Yeah, you will.

MUM. I won't. Abigail? I won't.

I'm gone.

Beat.

ABIGAIL. I'm not, though

MUM. Come here, love.

ABIGAIL. It's so unfair.

MUM. I know.

ABIGAIL. You shouldn't have gone yet

MUM. Surprise to me too, love.

ABIGAIL. Why do shit people have so much while the best…

MUM. I haven't always been the best though.

ABIGAIL. You have to me.

MUM. Not to your brother.

Beat.

Don't get into debt for me.

ABIGAIL. I'm fine.

MUM. What you gonna do about rent, bills?

ABIGAIL. I'll manage.

MUM. I don't want you to just manage, love

ABIGAIL. I don't mind.

MUM. Don't have me worrying from beyond the grave, cos I'll haunt you. I mean it.

ABIGAIL. I want you to haunt me.

MUM. You say that now but wait till three a.m. and I'm singing.

ABIGAIL. Haunt me. Please. I want you to haunt me.

Beat.

MUM. Phone the council.

ABIGAIL. I am not putting you in a grave with strangers.

MUM. Why not? I get on with everyone.

ABIGAIL. Mum.

MUM. Auntie Sue had a council burial, and it was actually quite nice. If anything, it was better, I could just cry without worrying how much it would cost me. All I want is for you and Darren to be there, together. I don't care who digs the hole.

ABIGAIL. What will people think of me though, Mum?

MUM. Who?

ABIGAIL. People

MUM. You'll have to narrow it down for me babe.

ABIGAIL. People walking past the cemetery.

MUM. Shouldn't be looking.

ABIGAIL. Your mates.

MUM. Most of my mates are dead or live in Spain, love.

ABIGAIL. My mates.

MUM. Since when have you cared what people thought you could afford and couldn't?

Beat.

ABIGAIL. I don't.

MUM. You must do to be doing this.

ABIGAIL. I want to do this.

MUM. So, you wanna say those things about me?

ABIGAIL. Of course not.

MUM. Then…?

ABIGAIL. I don't want you having a council burial

MUM. Why?

ABIGAIL. It's not…not…

MUM. Not what, Abs?

ABIGAIL. Dignified. I can't have people think I didn't love you.

MUM. Well if they see this darling they will, so what's the difference?

ABIGAIL. Can we talk about this later? Please?

Beat.

MUM. 'Ere, humour your ol' mum, one last time?

ABIGAIL. Why, you going somewhere?

MUM. Close your eyes, Abigail.

She does. MUM *stands by the exit.*

X Factor Champion, 2024 is… Drum roll…

ABIGAIL. Me.

ABIGAIL *opens her eyes and* MUM *is gone.*

Mum?

Beat.

DIRECTOR *calls.*

DIRECTOR. Can you give me that cue line again, please, Abs

She doesn't answer.

Abigail?

ABIGAIL. Sorry. It's my mum

DIRECTOR. Something wrong, Abs?

ABIGAIL. Yes. She died. Nineteen days ago.

A voicemail.

COUNCIL. Hello, Abigail, my name is Beth from the council funeral services. You, and Linda, have been refereed to me by the team at King's Hospital. Please try not to worry, my job here at the council is to help people like you, give their loved ones a dignified and fitting service, without the financial burden. I am currently supporting seven different families, so you are not alone. I know this time can be incredibly difficult, both emotionally and financially, I would love to speak to you, as soon as you can. It'd be great to hear all about Linda, you and Linda, her wishes, so I can begin arrangements. We do cremate as standard, unless Linda expressed alternative wishes...

ABIGAIL *picks up.*

ABIGAIL. She wants to be buried. She liked the fuss of a burial.

Beat.

ABIGAIL *stands by the grave,* DARREN *approaches.*

Does it look too deep to you?

DARREN. It's meant to be deep

ABIGAIL. Like really far away...

DARREN. They've probably got to fit another one in, Pebbles.

Sorry.

ABIGAIL. She never did like living on her own.

Beat.

DARREN. Service was nice. I liked the flowers.

ABIGAIL. They were left from the one before.

DARREN. Result. Did you wanna take them home?

ABIGAIL. Leave them for the next one.

Beat.

DARREN. It was a good turn-out

ABIGAIL. The celebrant said it was the best she'd seen, for one of these.

DARREN. That's something. I saw the Canning Town lot made the effort

ABIGAIL. Did they?

DARREN. Even Linda's second cousin Gillian was there

ABIGAIL. Gillian?

DARREN. The one who worked in the pie and mash shop with Linda. Didn't you say hello?

ABIGAIL. Nah, I didn't.

DARREN. I'll introduce you. She could tell you some stories about Linda. I said we'd meet them all down the pub for a drink

ABIGAIL. I'm gonna be busy here for a bit.

DARREN. There's nothing left to do, Pebbles

Beat.

ABIGAIL. I've got work tomorrow

DARREN. Always working. Still writing that play then?

ABIGAIL. I've got a double shift at the chippy.

Beat.

DARREN. Sorry, Pebbles.

ABIGAIL. Don't you wanna say I told you so?

DARREN. Why would I do that?

ABIGAIL. Because you did warn me. You said I wouldn't be able to.